FLUTE

Hymns FOR THE Master

15 FAVORITE HYMNS FOR SOLO PERFORMANCE

PLAYBACK+

Speed • Pitch • Balance • Loop

To access audio, visit:
www.halleonard.com/mylibrary

Enter Code
4691-8353-1630-9125

ISBN 978-0-7935-7186-4

HAL•LEONARD®

Copyright © 1996 by HAL LEONARD CORPORATION
International Copyright Secured   All Rights Reserved

Visit Hal Leonard Online at
www.halleonard.com

Contact us:
Hal Leonard
7777 West Bluemound Road
Milwaukee, WI 53213
Email: info@halleonard.com

In Europe, contact:
Hal Leonard Europe Limited
42 Wigmore Street
Marylebone, London, W1U 2RN
Email: info@halleonardeurope.com

In Australia, contact:
Hal Leonard Australia Pty. Ltd.
4 Lentara Court
Cheltenham, Victoria, 3192 Australia
Email: info@halleonard.com.au

ALL HAIL THE POWER OF JESUS' NAME

Flute

Traditional

JOYFUL, JOYFUL WE ADORE THEE

Flute

Traditional

TAKE MY LIFE AND LET IT BE

Flute

Traditional

GOD OF GRACE AND GOD OF GLORY

Text by HARRY EMERSON FOSDICK
Music by JOHN HUGHES

Flute

BE THOU MY VISION

Flute

Traditional Irish

CROWN HIM WITH MANY CROWNS

Flute

Traditional

I LOVE THEE

Flute

Traditional

ALL CREATURES OF OUR GOD AND KING

Flute

Traditional

broaden to end ———————— rit.

SAVIOR LIKE A SHEPHERD LEAD US

Flute

Traditional

MY FAITH LOOKS UP TO THEE

Flute

Traditional

JESUS SHALL REIGN WHERE'ER THE SUN

Words by ISAAC WATTS
Music by JOHN HATTON

Flute

THIS IS MY FATHER'S WORLD

Flute

Words by MALTBIE BABCOCK
Traditional Music

FOR THE BEAUTY OF THE EARTH

Text by FOLLIOT S. PIERPOINT
Music by CONRAD KOCHER

Flute

WHEN I SURVEY THE WONDROUS CROSS

Flute

Words by LOWELL MASON
Music by ISAAC WATTS

AMAZING GRACE

Words by JOHN NEWTON
Traditional American Melody

Flute

slower to ending   rit.